I0750292

FINISHING LINE PRESS
www.finishinglinepress.com

spare change

poems by

irene cooper

Finishing Line Press
Georgetown, Kentucky

spare change

ISBN 978-1-64662-452-2 First Edition

ACKNOWLEDGMENTS

"my purse is a tapestry bag…" took second place in the Oregon Poetry Association Spring Contest, 2016, experimental division

versions of "awakened to aching florescence" and "in basements," appear in Indolent Books' online project, *What Rough Beast*

versions of "felled baby bird" and "mother is a verb" appear in *Utterance: A Journal*

a version of "leeched of" appears in *The Feminist Wire*

a version of "to a certain nobody" appears in *Prometheus Dreaming*

versions of "i am cracked plate" and "a play of licorice" appear in *VoiceCatchers*

a version of "sometimes, in my perversity" appears in *phoebe*

versions of "the shore offers scarce evidence of us," "the difference between an albatross," and "the lord is on retreat" appear in *Cathexis Northwest Press*

Publisher: Leah Huete de Maines
Editor: Christen Kincaid
Cover Art: Brigitte Lewis, Artist
Author Photo: Irene Cooper
Cover Design: Elizabeth Maines McCleavy

Order online: www.finishinglinepress.com
also available on amazon.com

Author inquiries and mail orders:
Finishing Line Press
P. O. Box 1626
Georgetown, Kentucky 40324
U. S. A.

table of contents

in transit

salty morsels

late parade

in the snapshot
we line up
by age
look sideways
but for a sister
who
at the last second
faces the camera
head on
the world
in one moment
a shudder
of photo op
two-bit cyclone
in the next
a whip
lash of childhood
underfoot
hurled
where the dead
lie uncomposed
at most
illness is
a voracious
guest memory
hops on one leg
from the snapshot
we slip
the future a look

to a certain nobody:
a pair of wingtips is not
a means to fly   even if
you are not in love
with the lies of the father
the rain can be taken
for medicine   a boy has
seventy-two castanets
such doors seep
light in small doses
flush his golden hands

all incisors & milk
you are unassailable, knobbing up naked, singing
the hills alive, reservoir brimming at your back
best loved & creamy
mindless of cannibals in livery
                                        later, when every
eye is died, triumphant
blood rushes deaf to my ovation
  we're happy enough, most days

the body sere with treatment is fifteen
& yours is nine
what rules you subsumes you
though promise bursts like april dogwood
you artfully bloom,
                                        instead, like yeast
                                to swell the collapsed skin of him
let sacrifice be flesh alone   let the air of a body
never loved enough to be [inside]
wait inert for a late parade

ascending holy
linoleum stairs
you shadow
me like i'm
on my knees
before kiss
before i have
the next adonis
in my lip
line my dark
my breathless
doe eyed brother
i find you wanting
a faithless mouth
always racing
always slipping
a wet fish
to the slap
come a day
i'll lay
my idolatry
to rest
but the price
of monotheism
is empty rise
r is this passion
play of dumb

i can't shake
you & i
acted under
every circumstance
believe you
me, we
were mass produced—
urban icarus strung
melting o'er
flaming spires
i was the girl reporter
nicking copious notes
not in the hot seat
but not for want of fail
we of the caesarean
lift unmarked
unpassaged as dolls
& what of them wings?
how adept he is
they said
at folding them
just so
one molded
feather fell
& who knew
it was all of a piece
butter falls from a hot knife
just as we suspect
& glorious toast
the moment before coming
to, you
know the truth
about air
how easy it is to light
you were never so high
as the moony night
you burst into song

eyes tight to the last
i rise from the pit
to see you take leave
of your pooling
body
their scripted
triumph

at the shore we see scarce evidence of us
opened bodies deboned & ocean stripped

organs engaged in the kind of raw melody
you expect of cells free of their people suits

no secret tissue now too hot to poke
with a found liver with a length of carboned iris

unmixed & strung like clean kidneys in sunlight
it's almost better than drunk   this dissolution

morsels for gulls served fresh on a frigid
current of north atlantic insult   it feels good

to nourish something   you muck in the tide pools
fish out a heart-shaped rock   hand it to me

the difference between an albatross and a grappling hook is genre. the body beats up a hullabaloo to keep the mathematicians out of the liquor cabinet. until i see your bones reform i forget about the candles you light while everybody sleeps. between you and me, the only way to hear ourselves seep in peace is by cranking up the fiction. a loose tooth means i know you're away and can't take my call. in another life we are tusk to tusk in putrid battle, laughing and lifting our streaming nostrils to frighten the tourists. his brief pageant deprives us our banality. ark or gene pool, irony levels are dangerously high. what else goes into the water to keep us in stitches? your liquid body rolls off you like snake oil like thunder like the electric charge that siphons up the air.

leeched of
grace i rise
with ashes
in my mouth
from yes

pretty
thing sweet
fresh out of
sight put out
of mind your
manners love
some body
might hear

a child offering
coffee & cakes
to a priest
as you sleep

he empties
pockets of coins
& guilt
at the table
i come
clean

he lays
hands on
me as you
say no
thing

sometimes, in my perversity, i see our dead brother as a priest, see him peel back his black suit coat, release the button at his neck and take off his collar, lay it in a special bowl he keeps on his dresser. vain about his feet, he'll have traded the ugly brogans for motorcycle boots, an homage to the hippie priest that took him and his buddies to see *the summer of '42*, back when a girl washing her hair was pornography enough. shoes removed and down to his boxers now, hospital blue, he stands on his jesus feet—long bones and knuckles buckled with ache, encased in steaming argyle. i imagine our brother knows everything about sex from that movie, that day, as he accepts, when offered, a sip of water.

in basements
we wrenched lungs

of laundry detergent
& soot
                                        look

there's no sense
now

wagging our
forked livers
                        at our shame

& its con-
stituents

(the joists of us
warp under
                                the weight

clarity we carry
like a pane   of

glass between us
filmed soapy

& slipped
through   baby
                                fingers)

we salvaged
the frame

let's rest
our gaze on
                        some open

bent

she seizes that a body
in coma is a body in exodus
of sense none to know the permanence
of gone first blaze   then blackout
body without wake takes no measure
of the hours wiring downed & hissed
in possession of a systems failure
what she   she is   lies disembodied
a body's failure to respond   to be loved
on fire she walks to the sentient bed
passes through a score of felled days
no crumb no scrape of want   a smile
& mighty motor skills belie the notion
    she now seems different in the light

she now seems different in the light
bathed of morning dew dried gold
no flat florescence of hospital
no glow of casino   human moonless
and lonesome   by the slots in the ward
time is only distortion is only
a way to get paid   pores pour a light
of their own   skin a filter before
the coaling of organs on fire
no one really likes sundays—
the dim loathing of what weakness
                                                comes
but what day is it
when burst from the womb
child-shine   sunlight   the only sensible

child-shine sunlight the only sensible
action to be reckless with soak
fill every pore with honey
disinfectant   i spend our early
money on research & development
last night i dreamed of your death
you are big & the faults are mine
what chance & who gives   i leave everything
to me & can you forgive you   be honest
mistakes in no way are poetic
our most prosaic practice makes perfect
our scraps our chicken skin our late
with a cutting re-mark   brand us
with one honest word   c'mon
                                        impress me

with one honest word   come   impress (onto) me
your hot purity   permission to speak
to the open wound   if i drag a finger through
sucking ruts of what's done your backstory bobs
like a broken limb   lies like a roof on the lawn
a brackish pick-through   after a hurricane
named for an old flame   you won't remember
but you and I were at times kind   i love you less
for your strong back than for the tenderness
that pours from your eyes yes that shit   i'll say it
we were sad clowns   fearsome and early drowned—
you   juggling torches on your unicycle
i   hysterical in my fat suit—and without   some
fury bent on trashing every stage of us

fury   bent on trashing every stage of us
& in the wind a voice—*god don't be so*
                                        dramatic
& it's right i'm fine therapy saves just
                                        like jesus
we've a dog who loves her female pup
until it grows   & then she hates it—
an easy metaphor & anthropomorphic
i am a girl in the thick of middle age
i am a girl sworn to save her mother—
like baptism   a ceremony i can't recall
my part in
                the first & second son-deaths
i am unborn or deemed too uncomposed
                                        for funerals
when the third son-death   i stay home
pick a bone of grief for my own
                                        so selfish—
when i can hardly call you
                                        brother   her sun

when I could hardly call you brother her sun
articulates through me like latex like code
webbing my brain with her lovely face
we are not so very smart   using only
a tenth of our computers & then
only in pursuit of animal lush
                                        beauty is an angry god
and how can we live without god   my daughter
seizes at two still quaking at seven she says mama
this is about me taking care of myself
i lapse into coma at five   irreversibly wired
at twenty my daughter tells me at a distance:
you're too influential   but she's free—
fear only an aura of calamity   i sputter with relief
it's tiresome   this urging to believe

it’s tiresome   this urging to believe
in god   a better nature   me
i don’t care to speculate   then I do
i look at you & cogitate how you
carried it all in your skin coming in
you can only ever be disappointed
though ants have their charm
                                        we scream
feint at passing cars & monuments
& i can see you are your own deity
i am never so happy as at breakfast
when you & i feed our bodies
as though we love them
if there’s peace enough for you & me
to loiter after this it matters not a bit

to loiter after this   it matters not a bit
whether we click or don't click   clicking
is mechanics not karma   the whole
dead of bone cancer at fifteen
                    it's out of our pale will
we should have known by the soundtrack
we were set up despite your recent death
i think we might yet get along
like snow & flake
              if only language were so melting
the inebriate hastened toward death gifted
fetus to cell division   unique one moment
                                        to the next
beach weeds   what do we know of rivers
                                  & mammals
beyond the vanishing point we   who
practice chaos in panorama   in stills
in what i suspect is my life this diorama

in what i suspect is my life
this diorama
objets d'art block my view of the past
what does your feline spirit think
of the nonet?
how languorous weeks
spent inventing your infancy seemed
playing out your humanity
as you yielded
the bird to the bush left a field mouse
a leg to stand on
what fetal
decisions you made by my sick heart
beat
I evolve only enough to recognize
moments that eclipse meaning
i trust your will
with all my motherhood
spare spare change
is my new lodestar
my investment in everything
it's you who's taught me to believe & in nothing

it's you who's taught me to believe
                                        & in nothing
more than a veined defense of the dead
your son drank only on the weekends
you say   *how else could he make his living?*
                    so good for me, he was, so good
i am not
always sure which of your besotted
you lament   something like faith
buried with your husband
i come plain & empty handed to bait you
into some reflection past the picture frame
but shade and praise equally abrade
your hair looks nice i say
                                        i like those earrings
you ask about my husband's job
anything to keep the pleasantries in play

anything to keep the pleasantries in play
she holds silence like an open sore
a misery fox news trumpeting 24/7
can't mitigate the secret she leaks after
a year or so:
                              she sees the dead at bedside—
one tucks her in   another gapes like it's trying
to belch up her name a friend advises she firmly
tell the shadows to vamoose   but the wise move
might be to leave her to her spirits
the old man was visited by dogs
                                                            he'd get up
to let them out   hush the beasts so's not to bark
and wake her   in the daylight he'd forget
the interlude   smile when he rose & saw
the sliding door ajar bowl of water on the floor

the sliding door ajar
a bowl of water on the floor
a floor of needles in the yard
a yard of licorice in a jar
a bloom of pansies on the step
a can to water all the plants
to plant a step & then to wilt
a broken can a wound in bloom
the silence of a creeping cat
a canyon of a million sighs
a splay of bone the seep of hours
a next-door neighbor on the fence
a jar of sirens at the door
the play of licorice on the breath

the play of licorice on the breath
is everything i understand about desire
before coming to devotion. i watch a blue jay
charge its fledging, knock it from the fence
to force its flight. instead it sort of falls
into a low & prickly raspberry bush
as co-parent scans for crows, for cats
a kind of good/cop, bad/cop partnership.
our model was less experiential—love birds
danced in the kitchen, winged it, made passion
look easy as falling from a tree. thistle sharp
& hard to get to i'm more artichoke than avian,
grounded. but you, you drank up that sweet romance
like nectar, like medicine, like it was your job.

like nectar, like medicine, like it was your job
you tell jokes until the other brother snorts
soda out his nose, spit tobacco juice
between your teeth into a red solo cup
(curiously rural vice—you'd have some frail autonomy
with your poisons) your humor, indissoluble, is regular as night
it's your plaintive confession—an aside really
—that sober you have to learn afresh
how your household operates, your kids and all,
have to step back from these comets in motion
to see how best to shape yourself to their trajectory—
here I almost catch the toe of your mystifying faith,
to see that you, after so much masochistic macramé,
that you could, at the end, & for them, be loosed

she seizes that a body
she now seems different
                                        in the light
child-shine sunlight the only sensible
with one honest word   come
                                impress (onto) me
fury
     bent on trashing every stage of us
when I can hardly call you
                                  brother (her)
                                              sun
it's tiresome this urging to believe
to loiter
        after this it matters not a bit
in what i suspect is my life
                                  this diorama
it's you
          who's taught me to believe
anything
    to keep the pleasantries in play
the sliding door ajar
a play of licorice on the breath
like nectar   like medicine
                         like it was your job

in transit

the lord is on retreat working on his novel as we struggle with such language as is left us. i understand you are busy imploding. must be exhausted from always keeping us safe from happenstance, a diagnosis. i trip with three sedated cats and two more to a small room which becomes your absence. how can you hide now with innards exposed to the dawn. cue the chorus, so we know to weave laurels from the kale. your way of changing the subject to stone is winning. if you were here in this terrible moment you'd offer some medicinal bit of black. a horse walks into a bar. an elephant passes through a pane of glass. a sliding door is a measure of seeing while warm. how much can we river the water as it smells so poorly but swans. i have chipped my tooth on the laminate of this terrible moment and how will we walk this off with soles so cracked and blistered. three sedated cats awaken with hangovers, hungry with desire to paw the dogged jewel of you, casting stars across the ceiling and over the bedspread. night happens after everything. the word of our father turns to elegy, to emptied. who hears the clump leave his loosed grip but me.

you're wasted   from making your way
through la guardia to cascadia   this triage
a shunt for other duties   brief detour
from your real life   the work
that pushes   the wife & kids who pull
it's only our mother   who holds that first
loves last
she sips & smiles   expectant
of an anecdote   for this happy hour
you eschew the joke   spill instead
how hard it is to do with all the pills
how the pain erodes you   still
so little respite   in the end
you could always captivate
too late to stem
your surge she
muffles
her ears
to plug
the current
that would shock
her to her senses

i suggest
scenery
you like to drive
but prefer the cabin
    to
have more density
you want
    to
    you
    know
speed & brake
listen for the seconds
from the sirens to your *at*
sweep the grid
   winner
    take
     all
gentle bends undo you
if it's not game that's dear
who is necessary?
lone terrenaut
you shift
     on a road
        to
     nowhere
    a mountain
default talk
for thin air
a hawk silents about
how do you breathe
      you
      ask
all these trees

porta-potties   you pitch
for concerts   & vigils
you don't wink
& i'm strapped
holding your dream
like a cracked pipe
like a one-winged bird
your class of enthusiasm
hurts my eyes   it's no accident
waste management in this context
signifies your death   accelerant
you like a metaphor
hands & lies are optimistic
by nature   like treatment
like a book of addresses

you cover your body
in three-for-one serge—

you're not cheap   just dying
& pressed for time

                down to your thrift
you betray extravagance
—dropping sizes like change

at the sushi joint
you slather wasabi on sashimi
til blisters simmer your lip

tender ecstasy
i almost look away

finland is again the happiest country on earth, no wonder what with the sauna & jean sibelius, what with the hobbyhorses & vodka distilled with glacial spring water, silver birch that stipple a horizon like forsaken weapons. i watch scandinavian noir for the white space for the incomprehensible. dubbed voices are weirdly high in timbre. you drink swedish spirits until your body leaves you. sweden is ninth in happiness. your dedication to oblivion will be revealed as the fine handicraft it is, frigid absolut in fray.

we walk to the altar from the back of the church
—not the one that saves you
                                                            or swallows me
you walk with grace, bear the wine, the water
it must be me, then, who carries the host
unconsecrated over somber backs to the priest
a guy from the mediterranean, some island in dispute
these aisles, all of them, tiled coast to coast
like a klimt under my feet, not everlasting
—like this procession
                                              funny
how putting one foot in front of another becomes a ritual
in my parish in jersey, carrying the body and blood,
                                                            it's like you got to earn it,
you offer, as though we were in transit, or friends
any asshole can flip a twenty in the basket

i guess before your body turns to stone
tragedy comes wrapped in other colors
ash &   smoky azure on the bridge
end to end with feet   & disbelief
black bands for lifting golfers & civil
servants to their green end   again
the time to speculate on purpling is past
& since you can't know which blue bottle
will be the silver bullet you sport your sweet
golden self in violet jersey
white is the color of mourning
                                        & for men
in a red state   the women pink up
& the browning of children is considered
only sightly   in the end
a saturation of yellowing will illuminate
comets in trajectory   a soak of men

billowed skin does & does not betray
the beating you dedicate your life to
                                        your genius—
to juggle puns machined from ore to cool
how you pound boundaries so they don't appear
to warp   hubris to think no one thinks of roadkill
while seafaring   only the horizon   i know no pain
like the death of implicit
                                     an essay i skim is about you
from the point of view of god   my body knows
you're dead sunk but a lung is assailed by its hunger
by salt stilled winds & waters
we will never come about   you & i   flag our ships in this fog
bob in the shallows   say   here's this frothy thing
brings you to mind   oh hey next weekend   rig the kids   your wife
in a windless dream you drift   in irons   you laugh

magpie in mourning, the mother
asks a favor   as if never
                                        as if nothing
memory blazes with it now—
you square yourself to no
                                    and I can rub
my eye along the seam
of sever   a body reorganized
                                        you become
a man   at the brim   of bearing
bent to death   rent low
        a body of silence   fleet
        & lethal   as any preying owl

i watch my daughter swim
& in my windy chest
grace lights like rain on pollen
plastered   in the gravity of air
she blues she bleeds what is she
besides her soupy starts

the nothings i know of your children
i sponge from hearsay
how they do bloom from under the ice of us
can you see him now
red dusted lank of uniform
& progeny   a man without you
you echo on his tongue his song
a bird beyond your ashy grasp—

like my kid   soapy mirror
slipped phosphorescent
                    through my grip

i never make my mouth goodbye
you. you never lip it to me. i
eye you sideways, & don't nose. i mean
tonguing is tricky when shame swells
to spleen, fingers ache.

                                        we ear hello, after, say,
we stomach the cellular domestic
& can foot fall, erratic, toward a thank
of lunging.

           mind, you'll toe into hole, soon, skin you
shut, prick a tat of aperture, limning bilious pores
before blood shoulders you to sole.

salty morsels

awakened to aching florescence
i take note of the bars / wherever i am
my body pretends it's glad
to see me / surprised at the natural way
i lay open to the tide
i wake to see that as my brain / pine swept /
dissolves all the salty morsels on its tongue
you pray for death / i sleep /
out of kindness & a phobia of disorder   o
how will you tell me i was never your beloved

in this post-nuclear room
there are no heroes in league
            detachment perches
            on a shaky limb
performs its singular initiations
she swims the hot current
            beneath a blue
click of dolphins
teem of sharks
bowl of sandy
            flounder
            finning a cracked sink
to her glitter beds of shell
to her bottomless

my purse is a tapestry bag with a woven handle made from the sheath of a Yemeni janbiya, a blade used primarily for ceremonies and to eviscerate.

in a sweet
room a gloss
y albatross buz
zes into the void.
sudden husband sur
faces in breach
ed etiquette:

where r u?

infant day up
to the neck. mer
cury waxes muc
us recedes still
shoes stick to
their prom
ise to dig
narciss
us in no
vem
be
r
.

slipped of the caul & adept at
underwater breath she breaks
ancient from my thighs
                                        this before fall
now she keeps her seismology small
when she was a baby
i pared each fingernail as she slept
her rage a thrill
                                                like death
                                                to be held
at length it's funnier how she tells it
more cosmic joke than omen
the same animal but for timing
                                        a sum of parts
                                                and holes
hang by a thread   fault lines
ink her arm   map her drift

felled baby bird
not a metaphor

warmth in a palm
tissue in a purse

little histories of come
weight of a baby

bird in a brown
paper bag   a treat

maybe a sandwich
or the slack of still

feathers articulate
a pink belly & clean feet

it's a fact
your spiraled departures can't

whisk up enough juice
to enlighten the two of us

i wait in the dark much like before
my razored exit on the clock

fritter my one shot at privacy
when i lose consciousness what

code rewrote itself as i lay viral
what did scalp require of follicle

to replace it   & without me
your nose picks up its perfumes

like a lunatic   like an animal
like these hands of mine that can't
lie still

i am cracked plate   open-faced
fear serrated & tomato-fleshed
with the easy beatings of the underfed
i am whisked off my pickles guilt spins
me salt-beaded into my nightly
must my well-done my lean toward
bitter
          & suddenly the hot swirl of you
char & blister rustling up a brightness
so sizzle as to skitter rancid shame
& rue across its surface   distillate
& we are ancient eggs fermented
to ripeness we are vegetables in season
living mollusks on a nacred half-shell
all the briny sweet & sour of it

mother is a verb
do be do be do   the be
binds do to object, see,
so do can't do the doing—
buzz off, be, we're busy here
                                        got to

staunch the oozing scream
muffle the bellies
knit the bones to fly true
a score & more to
do be do be do the job, so be it

undone don't do
but to not be subject
is the object
apart from speech is do
& be is only the dream of her

prop open the noun
with a broom
free the chickens & shoot
for the treeline, no apples
in the pie, no gods

we buy a fish for the toddler

to teach about death
a tank is peaceful
as the grave
but for fluctuating
temperatures creeping
algae floundering
eye bulge in summer
when we ice the fish fry
but they die
they do
& so we engage our rituals
they are many they
                                        they are
piscine multitudes insistent
& pop mouthed
pleading no peace
                              twenty years
& edgar persists
a pale gourami—
sociable citizen fish—
who nevertheless commences
to eat five little fishes
birthed by a lost-named fish—
miracle of the tank—
& edgar is alone
swimming
& living
through new filters
foods fluorescent
bulbs of a particular length—
every administration
our daughter
                              no toddler
posits that this twitchy
hungry elder fish

this methuselah fish
is tied in life to grandma
but edgar dies at last
as fish do
utterly
& i who'd been indifferent
am slightly sad
& grandma's fine

the kinesiologist & the Sikh
inspire confidence   i
have to laugh
                                        at seven you become
a person who says she'll take care of herself
a stranger   the view from the bridge
is bottomless   fear
isn't that which flattens the arches—
it's the march   toward
a motion dependent on pull
                                                  let wonder
like every seizure you've swum to shore
be a commonplace

i can forgive a snowdrop
its precocity
having pushed
no push like that
since they caught the 2nd on the fly

we were slipped
& happy singing
a delicious scream
so elemental
so viscously new—
nothing so sweet since

spring is all that & not
so many as so many
whale songs are cold

fly dead
on the sill
            cold evidence
of my rainy
housekeeping

there is always monday
on its stony way

your absences
suspend clock
                & deliver
like november
snatched breath

betwixt ecstasy
                 & terror

an anecdote for this happy hour

there's this frothy thing that makes you come / hungry with desire to paw the dogged jewel of ~~you~~ me / [we are]unmarked unpassaged as dolls / lunatics so sizzle as to skitter rancid shame / [one]ocean stripped [to] two open bodies / best loved & creamy

acknowledgments

i am grateful for the people, both here and gone, who sit on the other side of and course through these conversations.

i am grateful to t.c. tolbert for early and unflagging support.

thank you, finishing line press, especially leah maines, kevin maines & christen kincaid, for yes.

thank you, brigitte lewis, again and again, and thank you beth alvarado, laura winberry, bella cooper, madeline cooper & michael cooper, by whom i am everyday enriched.

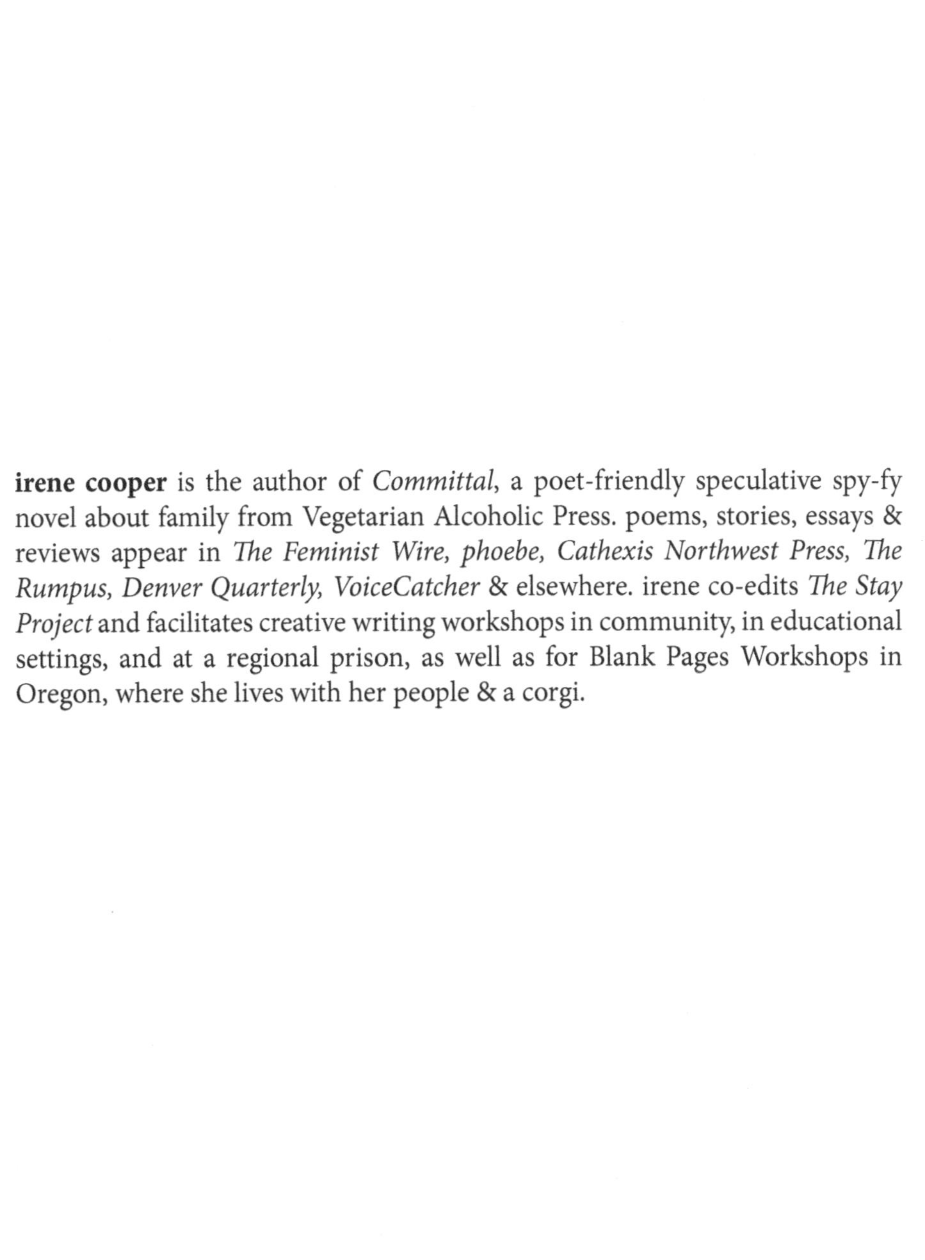

irene cooper is the author of *Committal*, a poet-friendly speculative spy-fy novel about family from Vegetarian Alcoholic Press. poems, stories, essays & reviews appear in *The Feminist Wire, phoebe, Cathexis Northwest Press, The Rumpus, Denver Quarterly, VoiceCatcher* & elsewhere. irene co-edits *The Stay Project* and facilitates creative writing workshops in community, in educational settings, and at a regional prison, as well as for Blank Pages Workshops in Oregon, where she lives with her people & a corgi.

www.ingramcontent.com/pod-product-compliance
Lightning Source LLC
LaVergne TN
LVHW051020080826
845145LV00009B/2713

* 9 7 8 1 6 4 6 6 2 4 5 2 2 *